Th MARRIAGE BOOK

The Rite of Marriage
for use in the
Dioceses of England and Wales

A Redemptorist Publication

The MARRIAGE BOOK
Published by:
Redemptorist Publications
A Registered Charity limited by guarantee. Registered in England 3261721

Editor: Francis Dickinson, C.SS.R.
This compilation ©1975 Redemptorist Publications

Fifty-seventh printing   June 2003 (372 thousand)

Concordat cum originali:
Fr John Dewis
July 1976

ISBN 0 85231 163 X

Printed by Lithgo Press Ltd., Leicester, LE8 6NU

Redemptorist
PUBLICATIONS
Alphonsus House Chawton Hampshire GU34 3HQ
Telephone 01420 88222   Fax 01420 88805
rp@ShineOnline.net   www.ShineOnline.net

The Rite of Marriage during Mass

Entrance Rite

The Priest may greet the Bride and Bridegroom at the church door and lead them with their parents and witnesses to the altar.

A HYMN may be sung (see pp 44-48) or the following Entry Antiphon may be said or sung:

**May the Lord send you help from heaven
and protect you from his citadel on high;
may he give you what your hearts desire,
and strengthen you in all you undertake.**

GREETING THE PEOPLE

All make the sign of the cross as the Priest says:

Priest: In the name of the Father, and of the Son, and of the Holy Spirit.

Congregation: **Amen.**

The Priest greets the People in one of these ways:

P: The grace of our Lord Jesus Christ and the love of God and the fellowship of the Holy Spirit be with you all.

or

The grace and peace of God our Father and the Lord Jesus Christ be with you.

or

The Lord be with you.

C: **And also with you.**

The Priest may now say a few words about the theme of the Nuptial Mass.

THE PENITENTIAL RITE

An Act of Penance follows, of which the following is one form:

P: My Brothers and sisters, (or some similar greeting) to prepare ourselves to celebrate the sacred mysteries, let us call to mind our sins:
(Pause, followed by these or similar invocations)

P: You were sent to heal the contrite:
Lord, have mercy.
C: **Lord, have mercy.**

P: You came to call sinners:
Christ, have mercy.
C: **Christ, have mercy.**

P: You plead for us at the right hand of the Father:
Lord, have mercy.
C: **Lord, have mercy.**

P: May almighty God have mercy on us,
forgive us our sins,
and bring us to everlasting life.
C: **Amen.**

THE GLORIA

The Gloria may be said on more solemn occasions.

P: Glory to God in the highest,

P & C: **and peace to his people on earth.**
Lord God, heavenly King,
almighty God and Father,
we worship you, we give you thanks,
we praise you for your glory.
Lord Jesus Christ, only Son of the Father,
Lord God, Lamb of God,
you take away the sin of the world:
have mercy on us;
you are seated at the right hand of the Father:
receive our prayer.

For you alone are the Holy One,
you alone are the Lord,
you alone are the Most High,
Jesus Christ,
with the Holy Spirit,
in the glory of God the Father. Amen.

COLLECT

The Priest now says, or sings, the Collect, of which the following is one form:

P: Let us pray.
(Pray silently for the Bride and Bridegroom)

Father,
you have made the bond of marriage
a holy mystery,
a symbol of Christ's love for his Church.
Hear our prayers for N. and N.
With faith in you and in each other
they pledge their love today.
May their lives always bear witness
to the reality of that love.
We ask you this
through our Lord Jesus Christ, your Son,
who lives and reigns with you and the Holy Spirit,
one God, for ever and ever.

C: **Amen.**

Liturgy of the Word

THE FIRST READING

The First Reading may be from the Old Testament or a non-Gospel one from the New Testament. At the end the Reader says:

R: This is the Word of the Lord.
C: **Thanks be to God.**

RESPONSORIAL PSALM

The Responsorial Psalm (of which the following is one form) is now said or sung. If said, the Reader leads it as follows:

R: The Lord fill the earth with his love.
C: **The Lord fills the earth with his love.**

R: They are happy, whose God is the Lord, the people he has chosen as his own. The Lord looks on those who revere him, on those who hope in his love.
C: **The Lord fills the earth with his love.**

R: Our soul is waiting for the Lord. The Lord is our help and our shield. In him do our hearts find joy. We trust in his holy name.
C: **The Lord fills the earth with his love.**

R: May your love be upon us, O Lord, as we place all our hope in you.
C: **The Lord fills the earth with his love.**

SECOND READING

There may be another reading before the Gospel. If so it ends as did the First Reading:
R: This is the Word of the Lord.
C: **Thanks be to God.**

ALLELUIA or ACCLAMATION

An Alleluia Versicle (during Lent, an Acclamation) may be said or sung. The following is one form of each:

Alleluia
C: **Alleluia, alleluia!**
God is love;
let us love one another
as God has loved us.
Alleluia!

Acclamation
C: **Anyone who lives in love**
lives in God,
and God lives in him.
Glory to you, O Christ,
you are the Word of God.

THE GOSPEL

Before reading the Gospel the Priest prays quietly:

P: Almighty God, cleanse my heart and my lips
that I may worthily proclaim your gospel.

Aloud, he says:
P: The Lord be with you.
C: **And also with you.**

P: A reading from the holy gospel according to N.
C: **Glory to you, Lord.**

At the end of the reading he says:
P: This is the gospel of the Lord.
C: **Praise to you, Lord Jesus Christ.**

Quietly, as he kisses the book:
P: May the words of the gospel wipe away our sins.

THE SERMON is preached.

Rite of Marriage

All stand, including the Bride and Bridegroom, and the Priest addresses them in these or similar words:

Priest: N. and N. (christian names only) you have come together in this church so that the Lord may seal and strengthen your love in the presence of the Church's minister and this community. Christ abundantly blesses this love. He has already consecrated you in baptism and now he enriches and strengthens you by a special sacrament so that you may assume the duties of marriage in mutual and lasting fidelity. And so, in the presence of the Church, I ask you to state your intentions.

The following questions are put once only, but the Bride and Bridegroom answer separately.

Priest: N. and N. (christian names only) I shall now ask you if you freely undertake the obligations of marriage, and to state that there is no legal impediment to your marriage.

Are you ready freely and without reservation to give yourselves to each other in marriage?

The Bridegroom answers first and then the Bride:

Bridegroom: **I am.**
Bride: **I am.**

Priest: Are you ready to love and honour each other as man and wife for the rest of your lives?
Bridegroom: **I am.**
Bride: **I am.**

The following question may be omitted if, for example, the couple is advanced in years.

Priest:	Are you ready to accept children lovingly from God, and bring them up according to the law of Christ and his Church?
Bridegroom:	**I am.**
Bride:	**I am.**

The BRIDEGROOM says after the Priest, or reads:

Bridegroom:	** **I do solemnly declare** **that I know not** **of any lawful impediment** **why I, N.N.** (full name, including surname), **may not be joined in matrimony** **to N.N.** (bride's full name, including surname).

Then the BRIDE says after the Priest, or reads:

Bride:	** **I do solemnly declare** **that I know not** **of any lawful impediment** **why I, N.N.** (full name, including surname), **may not be joined in matrimony** **to N.N.** (bridegroom's full name, including surname).

CONSENT

The Priest invites the couple to declare their consent:

Priest:	Since it is your intention to enter into marriage, declare your consent before God and his Church.

To the BRIDEGROOM:

Priest:	N.N., will you take N.N. here present for your lawful wife, according to the rite of our holy Mother the Church?
Bridegroom:	**I will.**

---

*These words are necessary for the civil validity of the marriage.

To the BRIDE:

Priest: N.N., will you take N.N. here present for your lawful husband, according to the rite of our holy Mother the Church?

Bride: **I will.**

The Bride and Bridegroom JOIN THEIR RIGHT HANDS. The Bride's hand may be placed in the Bridegroom's by the man who gives her away.

The BRIDEGROOM then says after the Priest, or reads:

Bridegroom: *I call upon these persons here present to witness
that I, N.N. (full name, including surname),
do take thee, N.N. (full name, including surname),
**to be my lawful wedded wife
to have and to hold from this day forward,
for better for worse, for richer for poorer,
in sickness and in health,
to love and to cherish,
till death do us part.**

They SEPARATE THEIR HANDS for a moment and then REJOIN THEM.

Then the BRIDE says after the Priest, or reads:

Bride: *I call upon these persons here present to witness
that I, N.N. (full name, including surname),
do take thee, N.N. (full name, including surname),
**to be my lawful wedded husband
to have and to hold from this day forward,
for better for worse, for richer for poorer,
in sickness and in health,
to love and to cherish,
till death do us part.**

---

*These words are necessary for the civil validity of the marriage.

Receiving their consent, the Priest says:

Priest: You have declared your consent before the Church. May the Lord in his goodness strengthen your consent and fill you both with his blessings.
What God has joined together, let no man put asunder.

All: **Amen.**

BLESSING AND EXCHANGE OF RINGS

The Priest now blesses the ring(s). The following is one form of the blessing:

Priest: May the Lord bless ✠ this ring (these rings)
which you give (to each other)
as the sign of your love and fidelity.

All: **Amen.**

The HUSBAND places his wife's ring on her finger, saying:

Husband: N. (christian name only), **take this ring as a sign of my love and fidelity. In the name of the Father, and of the Son, and of the Holy Spirit.**

If the husband is to receive a ring, the WIFE places it on his finger, saying:

Wife: N. (christian name only), **take this ring as a sign of my love and fidelity. In the name of the Father, and of the Son, and of the Holy Spirit.**

BIDDING PRAYERS

The Bidding Prayers (see selection pp 42-43) are said.

Each petition ends:

Reader: Lord, hear us.
All: **Lord, graciously hear us.**

The last petition may be made in these or similar words:

Reader: Let us commend ourselves and all God's people, living and dead, to Mary, Mother of God and wife of Joseph the carpenter.

All: **Hail, Mary, full of grace,**
the Lord is with thee.
Blessed art thou among women
and blessed is the fruit of thy womb,
** Jesus.**
Holy Mary, Mother of God,
pray for us sinners,
now and at the hour of our death.
Amen.

Reader: Let us now pray for a while in silence.

   (Pray silently)

Priest: Listen, O Lord,
to the prayers we offer for N. and N.
May their love for one another
be a never-failing reminder
of your own love for us all.
We ask this through Christ our Lord.
All: **Amen.**

THE CIVIL REGISTER

If necessary, the newly married couple, together with the witnesses, go to sign the civil register.

Liturgy of the Eucharist

A HYMN (see pp 44-48) may be sung, or the prayers offering the bread and wine may be said aloud. During the Offertory, the Bride and Bridegroom may bring the bread and wine to the altar.

As he offers the bread:

P: Blessed are you, Lord, God of all creation.
         Through your goodness we have this bread to offer,
         which earth has given and human hands have made.
         It will become for us the bread of life.
C: **Blessed be God for ever.**

Quietly, as he pours the wine and water into the chalice:

P: By the mystery of this water and wine
         may we come to share in the divinity of Christ,
         who humbled himself to share in our humanity.

As he offers the wine:

P: Blessed are you, Lord, God of all creation.
         Through your goodness we have this wine to offer,
         fruit of the vine and work of human hands.
         It will become our spiritual drink.
C: **Blessed be God for ever.**

Quietly, as he bows before the altar:

P: Lord God, we ask you to receive us
         and be pleased with the sacrifice we offer you
         with humble and contrite hearts.

Quietly, as he washes his hands:

P: Lord, wash away my iniquity;
         cleanse me from my sin.

He then addresses the Congregation:

P: Pray, brethren, that my sacrifice and yours
    may be acceptable to God, the almighty Father.
C: **May the Lord accept the sacrifice at your hands**
    for the praise and glory of his name,
    for our good, and the good of all his Church.

THE PRAYER OVER THE GIFTS

The Priest now says, or sings, the Prayer over the Gifts, of which
the following is one form:

P: Lord,
    accept our offering
    for this newly-married couple, N and N.
    By your love and providence you have
       brought them together;
    now bless them all the days of their married life.
    We ask this through Christ our Lord.
C: **Amen.**

The Eucharistic Prayer

P: The Lord be with you.

C: **And also with you.**

P: Lift up your hearts.

C: **We lift them up to the Lord.**

P: Let us give thanks to the Lord our God.

C: **It is right to give him thanks and praise.**

Preface No. 1

P: Father, all-powerful and ever-living God,
we do well always and everywhere to give you
    thanks.
By this sacrament your grace unites
    man and woman
in an unbreakable bond of love and peace.
You have designed the chaste love of husband
    and wife.
for the increase both of the human family
and of your own family born in baptism.
You are the loving Father of the world of nature;
you are the loving Father of the new creation
    of grace.
In Christian marriage you bring together the two
    orders of creation:
nature's gift of children enriches the world
and your grace enriches also your Church.
Through Christ the choirs of angels
and all the saints
praise and worship your glory.
May our voices blend with theirs
as we join in their unending hymn:

P & C: **Holy, holy, holy Lord, God of power and might,
heaven and earth are full of your glory.
    Hosanna in the highest.**

**Blessed is he who comes in the name of the Lord.
    Hosanna in the highest.**

Eucharistic Prayer I

(alternative: Eucharistic Prayer II, page 28)

We come to you, Father,
with praise and thanksgiving,
through Jesus Christ your Son.
Through him we ask you to accept and bless
these gifts we offer you in sacrifice.
We offer them for your holy catholic Church,
watch over it, Lord, and guide it;
grant it peace and unity throughout the world.
We offer them for N. our Pope,
for N. our bishop,
and for all who hold and teach the catholic faith
that comes to us from the apostles.

Remember, Lord, your people,
especially those for whom we now pray, N. and N.
        (Pray silently for the living)
Remember all of us gathered here before you.
You know how firmly we believe in you
and dedicate ourselves to you.
We offer you this sacrifice of praise
for ourselves and those who are dear to us.
We pray to you, our living and true God,
for our well-being and redemption.

Communicantes
In union with the whole Church
we honour Mary,
the ever-virgin mother of Jesus Christ our Lord and God.
We honour Joseph, her husband,
the apostles and martyrs
Peter and Paul, Andrew,
        *[James, John, Thomas,
        James, Philip,
        Bartholomew, Matthew, Simon and Jude;
        we honour Linus, Cletus, Clement, Sixtus,
        Cornelius, Cyprian, Lawrence, Chrysogonus,
        John and Paul, Cosmas and Damian]

and all the saints.

---

*[Sections in square brackets may be omitted throughout.]

May their merits and prayers
gain us your constant help and protection.
          [Through Christ our Lord. Amen.]

Hanc Igitur
Father, accept this offering
from your whole family
and from N. and N., for whom we now pray.
You have brought them to their wedding day:
grant them (*the gift and joy of children and)
a long and happy life together.
          [Through Christ our Lord. Amen.]

Bless and approve our offering;
make it acceptable to you,
an offering in spirit and in truth.
Let it become for us
the body and blood of Jesus Christ,
your only Son, our Lord.

The day before he suffered
he took bread in his sacred hands
and looking up to heaven,
to you, his almighty Father,
he gave you thanks and praise.
He broke the bread,
gave it to his disciples, and said:

Take this, all of you and eat it:
this is my body which will be given up for you.

When supper was ended,
he took the cup.
Again he gave you thanks and praise,
gave the cup to his disciples, and said:

Take this, all of you, and drink from it:
this is the cup of my blood,
the blood of the new and everlasting covenant.
It will be shed for you and for all
so that sins may be forgiven.
Do this in memory of me.

(* May be omitted whenever circumstances suggest it, if, for example, the couple
is advanced in years.)

P: Let us proclaim the mystery of faith:

The Congregation takes up one of these Acclamations:

1 **Christ has died,
Christ is risen,
Christ will come again.**

2 **Dying you destroyed our death,
rising you restored our life.
Lord Jesus, come in glory.**

3 **When we eat this bread and drink this cup,
we proclaim your death, Lord Jesus,
until you come in glory.**

4 **Lord, by your cross and resurrection
you have set us free.
You are the Saviour of the world.**

Father, we celebrate the memory of Christ, your Son.
We, your people and your ministers,
recall his passion,
his resurrection from the dead,
and his ascension into glory;
and from the many gifts you have given us
we offer to you, God of glory and majesty,
this holy and perfect sacrifice:
the bread of life
and the cup of eternal salvation.

Look with favour on these offerings
and accept them as once you accepted
the gifts of your servant Abel,
the sacrifice of Abraham, our father in faith,
and the bread and wine offered by your priest
     Melchisedech.

Almighty God,
we pray that your angel may take this sacrifice
to your altar in heaven.
Then, as we receive from this altar
the sacred body and blood of your Son,
let us be filled with every grace and blessing.
          [Through Christ our Lord. Amen.]

Remember, Lord, those who have died
and have gone before us marked with the sign of faith,
especially those for whom we now pray, N. and N.
          (Pray silently for the dead)
May these, and all who sleep in Christ,
find in your presence
light, happiness, and peace.
          [Through Christ our Lord. Amen.]

For ourselves, too, we ask
some shares in the fellowship of your apostles and
      martyrs
with John the Baptist, Stephen, Matthias, Barnabas,

      [Ignatius, Alexander, Marcellinus, Peter,
       Felicity, Perpetua, Agatha, Lucy,
       Agnes, Cecilia, Anastasia]

and all the saints.

Though we are sinners,
we trust in your mercy and love.
Do not consider what we truly deserve,
but grant us your forgiveness.

Through Christ our Lord
you give us all these gifts.
You fill them with life and goodness,
you bless them and make them holy.

Through him,
with him,
in him,
in the unity of the Holy Spirit,
all glory and honour is yours,
almighty Father,
for ever and ever,
C: **Amen.**

Communion Rite

THE LORD'S PRAYER

P: Let us pray with confidence to the Father
       in the words our Saviour gave us:

P & C: **Our Father, who art in heaven,**
hallowed be thy name.
Thy kingdom come.
Thy will be done on earth, as it is in heaven.
Give us this day our daily bread,
and forgive us our trespasses,
as we forgive those who trespass against us,
and lead us not into temptation,
but deliver us from evil.

THE NUPTIAL BLESSING

The Priest, facing the Bride and Bridegroom, gives the Nuptial Blessing, of which this is one form:

P: My dear friends, let us turn to the Lord and pray
       that he will bless with his grace this woman (or N.)
       now married in Christ to this man (or N.)
       and that *[through the sacrament of the body and
           blood of Christ,]
       he will unite in love the couple he has joined in this
           holy bond.
       (All pray silently for a short while)

■ In the following prayer, the Priest may choose the opening paragraph which corresponds to the reading of the Mass.

P: ■ Father, by your power you have made
               everything out of nothing.
       In the beginning you created the universe
       and made mankind in your own likeness.
       You gave man the constant help of woman
       so that man and woman should no longer be
               two, but one flesh,

---

*[May be omitted if one or both parties will not be receiving communion.]

and you teach us that what you have united
may never be divided.

■ Father, you have made the union of man and
    wife so holy a mystery
that it symbolizes the marriage of Christ and
    his Church.

■ Father, by your plan man and woman are united,
and married life has been established
as the one blessing that was not forfeited by
    original sin
or washed away in the flood.

Look with love upon this woman, your daughter,
now joined to her husband in marriage.
She asks your blessing.

Give her the grace of love and peace.
May she always follow the example of the holy
    women
whose praises are sung in the scriptures.

May her husband put his trust in her
and recognize that she is his equal
and the heir with him to the life of grace.
May he always honour her and love her
as Christ loves his bride, the Church.

Father, keep them always true to your
    commandments.
Keep them faithful in marriage
and let them be living examples of Christian life.
Give them the strength which comes from the
    gospel
so that they may be witnesses of Christ to others.
    *[Bless them with children
     and help them to be good parents.
     May they live to see their children's children.]
And, after a happy old age,
grant them fullness of life with the saints
in the kingdom of heaven.
We ask this through Christ our Lord.

C: **Amen.**

---

*[May be omitted whenever circumstances suggest it, if, for example, the couple
  is advanced in years.]

THE RITE OF PEACE

P: Lord Jesus Christ, you said to your apostles:
I leave you peace, my peace I give you.
Look not on our sins, but on the faith of your
  Church,
and grant us the peace and unity of your kingdom
where you live for ever and ever.

C: **Amen.**

P: The peace of the Lord be with you always.
C: **And also with you.**

The priest may now invite the people to greet one another.
P: Let us offer each other the sign of peace.

AGNUS DEI

The Agnus Dei is said or sung as the Priest takes the host, breaks
it and places a small piece in the chalice.

C: **Lamb of God, you take away the sins of the
  world:
have mercy on us.
Lamb of God, you take away the sins of the
  world:
have mercy on us.
Lamb of God, you take away the sins of the
  world:
grant us peace.**

The Priest prays quietly:

P: May this mingling of the body and blood
  of our Lord Jesus Christ
bring eternal life to us who receive it.

Then, either:

P: Lord, Jesus Christ, Son of the Living God,
by the will of the Father and the work of the
  Holy Spirit
your death brought life to the world.
By your holy body and blood
free me from all my sins and from every evil.

Keep me faithful to your teaching,
and never let me be parted from you.

or

P: Lord Jesus Christ,
with faith in your love and mercy
I eat your body and drink your blood.
Let it not bring me condemnation,
but health in mind and body.

HOLY COMMUNION

The Priest raises the host slightly and addresses the Congregation:

P: This is the Lamb of God
who takes away the sins of the world.
Happy are those who are called to his supper.

P & C: **Lord, I am not worthy to receive you,
but only say the word and I shall be healed.**

At his own Communion the Priest prays quietly:

P: May the body of Christ bring me to everlasting life.
May the blood of Christ bring me to everlasting life.

To each Communicant the Priest says:

Priest: The body of Christ.
Communicant: **Amen.**

If the Bride and Bridegroom receive under both kinds:

Priest: The blood of Christ.
Communicant: **Amen.**

A HYMN (see pp 44-48) may be sung, or a Communion Antiphon such as the following may be said or sung:

Christ loved the Church and sacrificed himself for her, so that she might be his holy and spotless Bride.

THANKSGIVING

After Communion a period of silence may be observed, or a Hymn (pp 44-48) may be sung

As he purifies the chalice, the Priest prays quietly:

P: Grant, Lord, that what we have received with
our mouth, we may accept with a pure heart;
and that from a temporal gift it may become for us
an everlasting remedy.

POST-COMMUNION

The Priest now says, or sings, the Post-communion
Prayer, of which the following is one form:

P: Let us pray.

(Pause, if there has been no period of silent prayer)

Lord
in your love
you have given us this eucharist
to unite us with one another and with you.
As you have made N. and N.
one in this sacrament of marriage
(and in the sharing of the one bread and the
   one cup),
so now make them one in love for each other.
We ask this through Christ our Lord.

C: **Amen.**

Concluding Rite

BLESSING AT THE END OF MASS

P: The Lord be with you.
C: **And also with you.**

Before blessing the people, the Priest blesses the Bride and Bridegroom, in a form such as the following:

P: God the eternal Father keep you in love for each
       other,
     so that the peace of Christ may stay with you
     and be always in your home.
C: **Amen.**

P: May (your children bless you,)
     your friends console you
     and all men live in peace with you.
C: **Amen.**

P: May you always bear witness to the love of God
       in the world
     so that the afflicted and the needy
     will find in you generous friends,
     and welcome you into the joys of heaven.
C: **Amen.**

He then blesses all present:

P: And may almighty God bless you all,
     the Father, and the Son, ✠ and the Holy Spirit.
C: **Amen.**

THE DISMISSAL

The Congregation is dismissed in one of the following forms:
P: Go in the peace of Christ.
       or
P: The Mass is ended, go in peace.
       or
P: Go in peace to love and serve the Lord.
C: **Thanks be to God.**

A HYMN (see pp 44-48) may be sung.

Eucharistic Prayer II

(for Eucharistic Prayer I, see page 18)

Lord, you are holy indeed,
the fountain of all holiness.
Let your Spirit come upon these gifts to make them holy,
so that they may become for us
the body and blood of our Lord, Jesus Christ.

Before he was given up to death,
a death he freely accepted,
he took bread and gave you thanks.
He broke the bread,
gave it to his disciples, and said:
Take this, all of you, and eat it:
this is my body which will be given up for you.

When supper was ended, he took the cup.
Again he gave you thanks and praise,
gave the cup to his disciples, and said:
Take this, all of you, and drink from it:
this is the cup of my blood,
the blood of the new and everlasting covenant.
It will be shed for you and for all
so that sins may be forgiven.
Do this in memory of me.

The Priest invites the Congregation:
P: Let us proclaim the mystery of faith:

The Congregation takes up one of these Acclamations:

1   **Christ has died,
Christ is risen,
Christ will come again.**

2   **Dying you destroyed our death,
rising you restored our life.
Lord Jesus, come in glory.**

3   **When we eat this bread and drink this cup,
we proclaim your death, Lord Jesus,
until you come in glory.**

4   **Lord, by your cross and resurrection
you have set us free.
You are the Saviour of the world.**

In memory of his death and resurrection,
we offer you, Father, this life-giving bread,
this saving cup.
We thank you for counting us worthy
to stand in your presence and serve you.
May all of us who share in the body and blood of Christ
be brought together in unity by the Holy Spirit.

Lord, remember your Church throughout the world;
make us grow in love,
together with N. our Pope,
N. our bishop, and all the clergy.
Remember our brothers and sisters
who have gone to their rest
in the hope of rising again;
bring them and all the departed
into the light of your presence.
Have mercy on us all;
make us worthy to share eternal life
with Mary, the virgin mother of God,
with the apostles,
and with all the saints who have done your will
   throughout the ages.
May we praise you in union with them,
and give you glory
through your Son, Jesus Christ.

Through him,
with him,
in him,
in the unity of the Holy Spirit,
all glory and honour is yours,
almighty Father,
for ever and ever.

C: **Amen.**

(Turn to page 22)

The Rite of Marriage outside of Mass

Entrance Rite

The Priest may greet the Bride and Bridegroom at the church door and lead them with their parents and witnesses to the altar.

A HYMN may be sung (see pp 44-48) or the following Entry Antiphon may be said or sung:

May the Lord send you help from heaven and protect you from his citadel on high: may he give you what your hearts desire, and strengthen you in all you undertake.

GREETING THE PEOPLE

All make the sign of the cross as the Priest says:

Priest: In the name of the Father, and of the Son, and of the Holy Spirit.

Congregation: **Amen.**

The Priest greets the People in one of these ways:

P: The grace of our Lord Jesus Christ and the love of God and the fellowship of the Holy Spirit be with you all.

or

The grace and peace of God our Father and the Lord Jesus Christ be with you.

or

The Lord be with you.

C: **And also with you.**

The Priest may now speak briefly about the celebration.

COLLECT

The Priest now says, or sings, the Collect, of which the following is one form:

P: Let us pray.
(Pray silently for the Bride and Bridegroom)

Father,
you have made the bond of marriage
a holy mystery,
a symbol of Christ's love for his Church.
Hear our prayers for N. and N.
With faith in you and in each other
they pledge their love today.
May their lives always bear witness
to the reality of that love.
We ask you this
through our Lord Jesus Christ, your Son,
who lives and reigns with you and the Holy Spirit,
one God, for ever and ever.

C: **Amen.**

Liturgy of the Word

THE FIRST READING

The First Reading may be from the Old Testament or a non-Gospel one from the New Testament. At the end the Reader says:

R: This is the Word of the Lord.
C: **Thanks be to God.**

RESPONSORIAL PSALM

The Responsorial Psalm (of which the following is one form) is now said or sung. If said, the Reader leads it as follows:

R: The Lord fills the earth with his love.
C: **The Lord fills the earth with his love.**

R: They are happy, whose God is the Lord, the people he has chosen as his own. The Lord looks on those who revere him, on those who hope in his love.
C: **The Lord fills the earth with his love.**

R: Our soul is waiting for the Lord. The Lord is our help and our shield. In him do our hearts find joy. We trust in his holy name.
C: **The Lord fills the earth with his love.**

R: May your love be upon us, O Lord, as we place all our hope in you.
C: **The Lord fills the earth with his love.**

SECOND READING

There may be another reading before the Gospel. If so it ends as did the First Reading:

R: This is the Word of the Lord.
C: **Thanks be to God.**

ALLELUIA or ACCLAMATION

An Alleluia Versicle (during Lent, an Acclamation) may be said or sung. The following is one form of each:

Alleluia
C: **Alleluia, alleluia!**
God is love;
let us love one another
as God has loved us.
Alleluia!

Acclamation
C: **Anyone who lives in love**
lives in God,
and God lives in him.
Glory to you, O Christ,
you are the Word of God.

THE GOSPEL

Before reading the Gospel the Priest prays quietly:

P: Almighty God, cleanse my heart and my lips
that I may worthily proclaim your gospel.

Aloud, he says:
P: The Lord be with you.
C: **And also with you.**

P: A reading from the holy gospel according to N.
C: **Glory to you, Lord.**

At the end of the reading he says:
P: This is the gospel of the Lord.
C: **Praise to you, Lord Jesus Christ.**

Quietly, as he kisses the book:
P: May the words of the gospel wipe away our sins.

THE SERMON is preached.

Rite of Marriage

All stand, including the Bride and Bridegroom, and the Priest addresses them in these or similar words:

Priest: N. and N. (christian names only) you have come together in this church so that the Lord may seal and strengthen your love in the presence of the Church's minister and this community. Christ abundantly blesses this love. He has already consecrated you in baptism and now he enriches and strengthens you by a special sacrament so that you may assume the duties of marriage in mutual and lasting fidelity. And so, in the presence of the Church, I ask you to state your intentions.

The following questions are put once only, but the Bride and Bridegroom answer separately.

Priest: N. and N. (christian names only) I shall now ask you if you freely undertake the obligations of marriage, and to state that there is no legal impediment to your marriage.

Are you ready freely and without reservation to give yourselves to each other in marriage?

The Bridegroom answers first and then the Bride:

Bridegroom: **I am.**
Bride: **I am.**

Priest: Are you ready to love and honour each other as man and wife for the rest of your lives?

Bridegroom: **I am.**
Bride: **I am.**

The following question may be omitted if, for example, the couple is advanced in years.

Priest: Are you ready to accept children lovingly from God, and bring them up according to the law of Christ and his Church?

Bridegroom: **I am.**
Bride: **I am.**

The BRIDEGROOM says after the Priest, or reads:

Bridegroom: * **I do solemnly declare**
that I know not
of any lawful impediment
why I, N.N. (full name, including surname),
may not be joined in matrimony
to N.N. (bride's full name, including surname).

Then the BRIDE says after the Priest, or reads:

Bride: * **I do solemnly declare**
that I know not
of any lawful impediment
why I, N.N. (full name, including surname),
may not be joined in matrimony
to N.N. (bridegroom's full name, including
surname).

CONSENT

The Priest invites the couple to declare their consent:

Priest: Since it is your intention to enter into marriage, declare your consent before God and his Church.

To the BRIDEGROOM:

Priest: N.N., will you take N.N. here present for your lawful wife, according to the rite of our holy Mother the Church?
Bridegroom: **I will.**

---

*These words are necessary for the civil validity of the marriage.

To the BRIDE:

| Priest: | N.N., will you take N.N. here present for your lawful husband, according to the rite of our holy Mother the Church? |
| Bride: | **I will.** |

The Bride and Bridegroom JOIN THEIR RIGHT HANDS. The Bride's hand may be placed in the Bridegroom's by the man who gives her away.

The BRIDEGROOM then says after the Priest, or reads:

| Bridegroom: | *I call upon these persons here present to witness
that I, N.N. (full name, including surname),
do take thee, N.N. (full name, including surname),
to be my lawful wedded wife
to have and to hold from this day forward,
for better for worse, for richer for poorer,
in sickness and in health,
to love and to cherish,
till death do us part. |

They SEPARATE THEIR HANDS for a moment and then REJOIN THEM.

Then the BRIDE says after the Priest, or reads:

| Bride: | *I call upon these persons here present to witness
that I, N.N. (full name, including surname),
do take thee, N.N. (full name, including surname),
to be my lawful wedded husband
to have and to hold from this day forward,
for better for worse, for richer for poorer,
in sickness and in health,
to love and to cherish,
till death do us part. |

---

*These words are necessary for the civil validity of the marriage.

Receiving their consent, the Priest says:

Priest:	You have declared your consent before the Church. May the Lord in his goodness strengthen your consent and fill you both with his blessings. What God has joined together, let no man put asunder.
All:	**Amen.**

BLESSING AND EXCHANGE OF RINGS

The Priest now blesses the ring(s). The following is one form of the blessing:

Priest:	May the Lord bless ✠ this ring (these rings) which you give (to each other) as the sign of your love and fidelity.
All:	**Amen.**

The HUSBAND places his wife's ring on her finger, saying:

Husband:	**N.** (christian name only), **take this ring as a sign of my love and fidelity. In the name of the Father, and of the Son, and of the Holy Spirit.**

If the husband is to receive a ring, the WIFE places it on his finger, saying:

Wife:	**N.** (christian name only), **take this ring as a sign of my love and fidelity. In the name of the Father, and of the Son, and of the Holy Spirit.**

BIDDING PRAYERS

The Bidding Prayers (see selection pp 42-43) are said.

Each petition ends:

Reader:	Lord, hear us.
All:	**Lord, graciously hear us.**

The last petition may be made in these or similar words:

Reader: Let us commend ourselves and all God's people, living and dead, to Mary, Mother of God and wife of Joseph the carpenter.

All: **Hail, Mary, full of grace,**
the Lord is with thee.
Blessed art thou among women
and blessed is the fruit of thy womb,
Jesus.
Holy Mary, Mother of God,
pray for us sinners,
now and at the hour of our death.
Amen.

Reader: Let us now pray for a while in silence.

(Pray silently)

THE NUPTIAL BLESSING

The Priest gives the Nuptial Blessing, of which the following is one form. He chooses the opening paragraph which corresponds to the reading.

P: ■ Father, by your power you have made
everything out of nothing.
In the beginning you created the universe
and made mankind in your own likeness.
You gave man the constant help of woman
so that man and woman should no longer be
two, but one flesh,
and you teach us that what you have united
may never be divided.

■ Father, you have made the union of man and
wife so holy a mystery
that it symbolizes the marriage of Christ and
his Church.

■ Father, by your plan man and woman are united,
and married life has been established
as the one blessing that was not forfeited by
original sin
or washed away in the flood.

Look with love upon this woman, your daughter,
now joined to her husband in marriage.
She asks your blessing.

Give her the grace of love and peace.
May she always follow the example of the holy
    women
whose praises are sung in the scriptures.

May her husband put his trust in her
and recognize that she is his equal
and the heir with him to the life of grace.
May he always honour her and love her
as Christ loves his bride, the Church.

Father, keep them always true to your
    commandments.
Keep them faithful in marriage
and let them be living examples of Christian life.
Give them the strength which comes from the
    gospel
so that they may be witnesses of Christ to others.
    *[Bless them with children
      and help them to be good parents.
      May they live to see their children's children.]
And, after a happy old age,
grant them fullness of life with the saints
in the kingdom of heaven.
We ask this through Christ our Lord.

C: **Amen.**

---

*[May be omitted whenever circumstances suggest it, if, for example, the couple is advanced in years.]

Conclusion of the Celebration

THE LORD'S PRAYER

P: Let us pray with confidence to the Father
in the words our Saviour gave us:

P & C: **Our Father, who art in heaven,**
hallowed be thy name.
Thy kingdom come.
Thy will be done on earth, as it is in heaven.
Give us this day our daily bread,
and forgive us our trespasses,
as we forgive those who trespass against us,
and lead us not into temptation,
but deliver us from evil.

HOLY COMMUNION

Holy Communion may be distributed. The Priest holds
up a host and addresses the Congregation:

P: This is the Lamb of God
who takes away the sins of the world.
Happy are those who are called to his supper.

P & C: **Lord, I am not worthy to receive you,**
but only say the word and I shall be healed.

To each Communicant the Priest says:

Priest: The body of Christ.
Communicant: **Amen.**

THANKSGIVING

After Communion a period of silence may be observed.
or a Hymn (pp 44-48) may be sung. Then a Prayer
such as the following may be said:

P: Let us pray.
Lord, we who have shared the food of your
table
pray for our friends, N. and N.
whom you have joined together in marriage.
Keep them close to you always.
May their love for each other

proclaim to all the world
their faith in you.
We ask this through Christ our Lord.
C: **Amen.**

THE FINAL BLESSING

P: The Lord be with you.
C: **And also with you.**

Before blessing the people, the Priest blesses the Bride and Bridegroom, in a form such as the following:

P: God the eternal Father keep you in love for each
    other,
so that the peace of Christ may stay with you
and be always in your home.
C: **Amen.**
P: May (your children bless you,)
your friends console you
and all men live in peace with you.
C: **Amen.**
P: May you always bear witness to the love of God
    in the world
so that the afflicted and the needy
will find in you generous friends,
and welcome you into the joys of heaven.
C: **Amen.**

He then blesses all present:
P: And may almighty God bless you all,
the Father, and the Son, ✠ and the Holy Spirit.
C: **Amen.**

THE DISMISSAL

The Congregation is dismissed in one of the following forms:

P: Go in the peace of Christ.
    or
P: Go in peace to love and serve the Lord.
C: **Thanks be to God.**

THE CIVIL REGISTER

The newly married couple, together with the witnesses, go to sign the civil register.

A HYMN (see pp 44-48) may be sung.

Appendix: Bidding Prayers

Any appropriate bidding prayers may be said. Some or all of those given here may be used, or others specially composed for the occasion.

Priest: In the love of man and wife, God shows us a wonderful reflection of his own eternal love. Today   N. and N. have dedicated themselves to one another in unending love. They will share with one another all that life brings. Let us ask God to bless them in the years ahead, and to be with them in all the circumstances of their marriage.

Reader: Christ is present to N. and N. in this Sacrament of Matrimony. We pray that he will continue to make his presence felt throughout their lives.
Lord, hear us.

1

People: **Lord, graciously hear us.**

Reader: May the grace given to N. and N. in this Sacrament of Matrimony be always active in them. May it inspire them when life seems dull and strengthen them in times of trial. May it give them understanding in moments of tension, and fill them with gratitude when all goes well.
Lord, hear us.

2

People: **Lord, graciously hear us.**

Reader: May the love of N. and N. grow large enough to embrace the children God may send them. May they, in their turn, bring ever greater happiness to their parents.
Lord, hear us.

3

People: **Lord, graciously hear us.**

Reader: By this marriage our two families have been united. May all of us, and particularly the parents of N. and N., increase in affection for one another, and find in one another a source of help and strength.
Lord, hear us.

4

People: **Lord, graciously hear us.**

Reader:

5

May we learn to value the ideals and beliefs of others. May the love and understanding of our families bring nearer the day Christ prayed for, when there shall be only one flock and one shepherd.
Lord, hear us.

People: **Lord, graciously hear us.**

Reader:

6

We pray for all the friends of N. and N. We pray especially for those who have had some part in bringing them to this happy day. May God bless them with the gift of his own undying friendship.
Lord, hear us.

People: **Lord, graciously hear us.**

Reader:

7

May all married people here with us be reminded of the joy of their own wedding day. May they give thanks for all the happiness they have known. May each day find them ever more devoted to one another.
Lord, hear us.

People: **Lord, graciously hear us.**

Reader:

8

We pray for those of our dear ones who have departed this life. May God give them eternal rest.
Lord, hear us.

People: **Lord, graciously hear us.**

Marriage during Mass: turn to page 14.

Marriage outside of Mass: turn to page 38.

HYMNS

All these hymns may be sung to familiar tunes

1 Praise, my soul, the
 king of heaven;
to his feet thy tribute bring.
Ransomed, healed, restored,
 forgiven,
who like me his praise
 should sing?
Praise him! Praise him!
Praise him! Praise him!
Praise the everlasting king.

2.
Praise him for his grace and
 favour
to our fathers in distress;
praise him still the same for
 ever,
slow to chide and swift to
 bless.
Praise him! Praise him!
Praise him! Praise him!
Glorious in his faithfulness.

3.
Father-like, he tends and
 spares us;
well our feeble frame he
 knows;
in his hands he gently
 bears us,
rescues us from all our foes.
Praise him! Praise him!
Praise him! Praise him!
Widely as his mercy flows.

4.
Angels, help us to adore him;
ye behold him face to face;
sun and moon, bow down
 before him;
dwellers all in time and space.
Praise him! Praise him!
Praise him! Praise him!
Praise with us the God of
 grace.

2 All people that on
 earth do dwell,
sing to the Lord, with
 cheerful voice;
him serve with mirth, his
 praise forth tell,
come ye before him, and
 rejoice.

2.
The Lord, ye know, is God
 indeed;
without our aid he did us
 make;
we are his folk, he did us
 feed,
and for his sheep he doth
 us take.

3.
O enter then his gates with
 praise;
approach with joy his
 courts unto;
praise, laud and bless his
 name always,
for it is seemly so to do.

4.
For why, the Lord our God is
 good:
his mercy is for ever sure;
his truth at all times firmly
 stood,
and shall from age to age
 endure.

5.
To Father, Son, and Holy
 Ghost.
the God whom heaven and
 earth adore,
from men and from the
 angel-host
be praise and glory
 evermore.

HYMNS

3 O God, we give
ourselves today
with this pure host to thee,
the selfsame gift which thy
  dear Son
gave once on Calvary:

2.
Entire and whole, our life and
  love
with heart and soul and mind,
for all our sins and faults and
  needs,
thy Church and all mankind.

3.
With humble and with
  contrite heart
this bread and wine we give,
because thy Son once gave
  himself
and died that we might live.

4.
Though lowly now, soon by
  thy word
these offered gifts will be
the very body of our Lord,
his soul and deity.

5.
His very body, offered up,
a gift beyond all price,
he gives to us, that we may give
in loving sacrifice.

6.
O Lord, who took our human
  life,
as water mixed with wine,
grant through this sacrifice
  that we
may share thy life divine.

4 O King of might and
splendour,
creator most adored,
this sacrifice we render
to thee as sovereign Lord.
May these, our gifts, be
  pleasing
unto thy majesty,
mankind from sin releasing
who have offended thee.

2.
Thy body thou hast given,
thy blood thou hast
  outpoured,
that sin might be forgiven,
O Jesu, loving Lord.
As now with love most tender
thy death we celebrate,
our lives in self-surrender
to thee we consecrate.

HYMNS

5 O bread of heaven, beneath this veil
thou dost my very God conceal:
my Jesus, dearest treasure, hail;
I love thee and adoring kneel;
each loving soul by thee is fed
with thy own self in form of bread.

2.
O food of life, thou who dost give
the pledge of immortality;
I live; no, 'tis not I that live;
God gives me life, God lives in me:
he feeds my soul, he guides my ways,
and every grief with joy repays.

3.
O bond of love, that dost unite
the servant to his living Lord;
could I dare live and not requite
such love, – then death were meet reward:
I cannot live unless to prove
some love for such unmeasured love.

4.
Beloved Lord in heaven above,
there, Jesus, thou awaitest me;
to gaze on thee with changeless love;
yes, thus I hope, thus shall it be:
for how can he deny me heaven
who here on earth himself hath given?

6 I am not worthy, holy Lord,
that thou shouldst come to me:
speak but the word; one gracious word
can set the sinner free.

2.
I am not worthy; cold and bare
the lodging of my soul;
how canst thou deign to enter there?
Lord, speak, and make me whole.

3.
I am not worthy; yet, my God,
how can I say thee nay;
thee, who didst give thy flesh and blood
my ransom-price to pay?

4.
O come! in this our joyful hour,
feed me with food divine;
and fill with all thy love and power
this worthless heart of mine.

HYMNS

7 Love divine, all loves
    excelling,
joy of heaven, to earth come
  down,
fix in us thy humble dwelling,
all thy faithful mercies crown.

2.
Jesus, thou art all
  compassion,
pure unbounded love thou
  art;
visit us with thy salvation,
enter every trembling heart.

3.
Come, almighty to deliver,
let us all thy life receive;
suddenly return, and never,
never more thy temples
  leave.

4.
Thee we would be always
  blessing,
serve thee as thy hosts
  above;
pray, and praise thee
  without ceasing,
glory in thy perfect love.

5.
Finish then thy new
  creation
pure and sinless let us be;
let us see thy great
  salvation,
perfectly restored in thee.

6.
Changed from glory into
  glory,
till in heaven we take our
  place,
till we cast our crowns
  before thee,
lost in wonder, love and
  praise.

8 Praise we our God
    with joy
and gladness never ending;
angels and saints with us
their grateful voices
  blending.
He is our Father dear,
o'erfilled with parent's love;
mercies unsought,
  unknown,
he showers from above.

2.
He is our shepherd true;
with watchful care
  unsleeping,
on us, his erring sheep,
an eye of pity keeping;
he with a mighty arm
the bonds of sin doth break,
and to our burdened hearts
in words of peace doth
  speak.

3.
Graces in copious stream
from that pure fount are
  welling,
where, in our heart of
  hearts,
our God hath set his
  dwelling.
His word our lantern is,
his peace our comfort still,
his sweetness all our rest,
our law, our life, his will.

HYMNS

9

Father, within thy
house today
we wait thy kindly love
to see:
since thou hast said in
truth that they
who dwell in love are one
with thee,
bless those who for thy
blessing wait;
their love accept and
consecrate.

2.

Blest Spirit, who with life
and light
didst quicken chaos to thy
praise,
whose energy, in sin's
despite,
still lifts our nature up to
grace,
bless those who here in
troth consent.
Creator, crown thy
sacrament.

3.

Great one in thee, of whom
are named
all families in earth and
heaven,
hear us, who have thy
promise claimed,
and let a wealth of grace be
given;
grant them in life and
death to be
each knit to each, and both
to thee.

10

The Lord's my
Shepherd,
I'll not want;
he makes me down to lie
in pastures green:
he leadeth me
the quiet waters by.

2.

My soul he doth
restore again;
and me to walk doth
make
within the paths
of righteousness
ev'n for his own name's
sake.

3.

Yea, though I walk
in death's dark vale,
yet will I fear none ill:
for thou art with me;
and thy rod
and staff me comfort still.

4.

My table thou
hast furnished
in presence of my foes.
My head thou dost
with oil anoint
and my cup overflows.

5.

Goodness and mercy
all my life
shall surely follow me:
and in God's home
for evermore
my dwelling-place shall
be.